Secrets Of The Body

# FRANK DULLAGHAN
# Secrets Of The Body

A sequence of poems on the life of Pope Joan

**EYEWEAR**  **AVIATOR**

2016 SERIES

First published in 2016
by Eyewear Publishing Ltd
Suite 333, 19-21 Crawford Street
Marylebone, London W1H 1PJ
United Kingdom

**Typeset with graphic design by** Edwin Smet
**Cover and author painting by** Aidan Dullaghan
**Printed in England by** Lightning Source
**All rights reserved** © 2016 Frank Dullaghan

The right of Frank Dullaghan to be identified as author of this work has been asserted in accordance with section 77 of the Copyright, Designs and Patents Act 1988

ISBN 978-1-911335-09-2

*Eyewear wishes to thank Jonathan Wonham for his generous patronage of our press.*

WWW.EYEWEARPUBLISHING.COM

*I would like to dedicate*
*this pamphlet to the special women in my life*

To my wife, Marie,
for this long journey we share

To my daughter-in-law, Lynsey
for being bright and beautiful

To my youngest son's partner, Louise,
for being more than a pretty face

To my great and close friend, Zeina,
for being the best poet I know

To Mary and Rosemarie
for being my sisters

To my granddaughter Holly
for being Holly

# TABLE OF CONTENTS

8   HISTORICAL NOTE

10   FLIGHT
11   AGNES
13   DRESSED IN A NAME
14   THE DOLL
15   THE HORSEMAN
16   A SOLDIER'S BLESSING
17   RAGE
18   IN THE WORLD OF MEN
19   SPYING
20   STAIRS
21   THE UNBROKEN LINE
22   THE SECRETS OF THE BODY
23   WHAT STRANGENESS
24   UNLOCKED
25   BREAD
26   A LOVE LIKE THIS
27   THE COMING STORM
28   I AM
29   BIG
30   AFTERWARDS
31   EXPURGATED
32   CANDLE

33   ACKNOWLEDGEMENTS

# HISTORICAL NOTE

According to the legends, a baby girl was born in the 9th century (some accounts place the date as late as the early 12th century) to English parents who were missionaries in Germany. She was named Agnes in some accounts. Rebelling against the medieval laws forbidding women to study and learn, she disguised herself as a boy and entered Fulda, a Benedictine monastery, under the name of John. This name may have been her brother's name. He is said to have been brutally killed during a Viking attack or in an altercation of some sort.

She studied for a while in Greece before coming to the attention of the Vatican where she became a notary to the Curia, then cardinal and finally the Pope. She is said to have headed the Church from 855 until 858. In the legends she was given the name Joan, the feminine form of John.

According to legend, she is said to have had a lover and to have become pregnant by him, leading to her discovery as a woman. In some accounts, she gave birth whilst in procession from St. Peter's to the Lateran, somewhere between the Colosseum and St. Clement's. She is supposed to have been either stoned to death by the crowd or tied to a horse and dragged through the streets. In processions through Rome, the Popes always avoid this road. Many believe that they do this out of abhorrence of that event. Others say that it is simply because the road is very narrow.

In other accounts, she was quietly sent to a convent. Her child, a boy, became Bishop of Ostia and then a cardinal. He is said to have had her bones moved to his cathedral and interred there. Versions of the legend were only recorded during the Middle Ages. The most widely accepted version is by Martin of Troppau (Martinus Polonus), a Dominican friar in Poland, and was written in 1265. The Church has denied the existence of a female pope, stating that it was Protestant propaganda and that there are no accounts from the supposed time of her reign. Other researchers, however, say that there are plenty of pre-Reformation Catholic texts which mention a female pope and that the full story was orally passed down and accepted within the Catholic Church until it became an embarrassment during the Reformation. They claim that Church records were altered at the time, to hide the facts. Whatever the truth of the legend, it provides an intriguing story.

# FLIGHT

A bird should never be held
in a cage with its wings clipped,
admired for its voice, for its grace,
be told that the world is too wide,
that only men may wander, learn,
that the only language it needs
is its song, the only knowledge,
to respect the hand that feeds it.
You'd think that God had not already
given it the sky, told it to fly.

# AGNES

Why does God smile differently on men,
paths are cleared, gates opened, their journey
less of a struggle? I'm no different in my head.
I can see the pastures to be entered
but not the way. Fence posts
stand like soldiers set against me.

My sullen brother is sent to school
with bread and coin to gad about, take little
learning in. I scour for opportunities –
my letters from the village signs and
an old man minding sheep who would
show off, if only to a girl.

They want to marry me to a bony man
who owns a horse. I know it was his cousin's,
a man who fell in the mountain where this one would
never go. Now he's blessed with someone else's
value, he wears it like his own.
All say how smart he is, how enterprising.

I know him as an upstart who would grind me down.
The only coin of trade I own is my soft body.
I know enough to know its value will not last
nor the trade be worth the cost. Yet if I stay,
the bony man will have it all for free
and two pairs of goats as dowry.

So I will be a boy and take a different road.
There's work, I've heard, and board in the monastery.
They are miserly with their coin

but that's not what I want.
There's knowledge there that I can pilfer
as I grow into a man.

## DRESSED IN A NAME

When word came that John had died –
an altercation on the ale-house road –
great lamentation reigned within our home.
For brave John was the one my father said would go
to Fulda, study for the priesthood there and
bring great learning, wealth and honour
by return.

The door was hung in black; my father wept
and cursed to have no son. I was banished
to an aunt and took the chance I had
to don the good John's clothes and take his name.
He would never have survived the monastery,
having no sobriety or subtlety of wit.
They expect a John to knock upon their door.
They'll let me in.

# THE DOLL

It was hardly a doll – sackcloth and buttons,
twine weaved into the head and
hanging in unlovely tendrils.
But above where the heart would be
a little red daisy was embroidered,
the only colour it had.
It seemed discarded or lost.
I'd picked it up from the path absent-mindedly
when I was passing with my brothers.
We examined it and smiled weakly:
the girl it came from was obviously as poor
as the doll was made. I carried it to my cell
unthinking. Or rather, thinking
of the philosophical debate we had had
on the nature of reality.
I placed it on a stool next to the wall.
When I stooped to examine the embroidery,
the obvious care taken there, I wept
as if I had been the one to lose it.

# THE HORSEMAN

A horseman rode in and word came
that he'd been sent to find me.
His horse stamped and snorted in the yard
as my brothers unsaddled it. The abbot
dined with the rider before he called for me.

I am to go to Rome to work for the Curia.
I had not meant to draw attention to myself
but my love of knowledge is like a light
that won't go out. It would seem
it shone all the way to the Vatican.

Now this man with such cool blue eyes, such
interesting hands, is to be my companion
on the road. In the yard they are readying
a mount for me. I can feel the horseman's
eyes on the soft nape of my neck.

## A SOLDIER'S BLESSING

There was something about this man's stance
that was different. I could see he was a soldier.

His face wore a hardness that made one step aside,
even though he was not in his leathers and iron.

I watched how quickly he formed opinion
behind the dark of his eyes, how he reached judgment

privately and needed no counsel, respecting
only his own. His life, I decided, was a treasure

he carried daily and so he understood its value,
his need to protect it, to be beholden to no one.

In this, I think, he might have been closer to God
than we of the cloth, who place all value

in the sound of our own voices complicating
everything. His hands looked tidy, capable.

I was struck by the thought that if I were to be blessed,
his would be the hands I would want to do it.

# RAGE

I dreamt I flew home on a wind.
The door was half-open, it being still
the afternoon. I saw how small
the house was, how soiled with age.

A stray dog slunk under the window,
looked my way then darted off,
its skinny body trembling.
I stepped into the front room

with its heavy table, its dresser.
My father was in a storm of rage,
the walls flung themselves back
from his roars. There was blood

on my mother's face. Everything was
the same. I understood, as I always had,
that he screamed out of his ignorance.
He had been taken for a fool again

and healed his wounded manhood
by breaking the soft body of my mother.
I cried out, as I always had. But this time,
when he looked, his fire didn't burn me.

Instead, he fell to his knees
and blessed himself. *Forgive me, Father,*
he pleaded. *You are asking
the wrong person,* I told him.

# IN THE WORLD OF MEN

We are men of God. Even I.
We have clean hands and clean feet.
We bathe when we need and we eat
every day. Each night we lie

in a bed. We live such a life
yet we brand and we scourge,
we flay, we rack and we gauge,
so sure are we in belief.

*What if we're wrong?* I ask
my brothers, *what if we're deaf
to the voice of Our Lord, to His gift?
What if we're blind to the task*

*He has set us?* Love has no part
in the gospel we preach.
We would hammer all into Heaven, reach
with a sword for their heart.

*It is the will of our Holy Father.*
And that is enough, they suppose.
There's no reasoning with those
who believe they know better.

# SPYING

The Cardinal's spy confessed once
over wine, that most times he escaped
detection by dressing as a woman.
*To be convincing, he said, is not*
*just a matter of padded clothes, a way*
*of moving. You need, also, to inhabit*
*the female mind.* I told him I had no clue
how one could do this. *You must don*
*an attitude of servitude,* he said,
*be timid, always lower your gaze, avoid*
*uncrowded places, never step out first,*
*hold all men in the greatest of suspicions.*
It must be difficult, I said. *It would never*
*work for you,* he said, *your mind*
*is too bold, you have insufficient fear.*
Women, he said, *are too alien to you.*
*You would make a poor one.* I agreed.

# STAIRS

It has always been my nature to chase ideas.
I nurture them the way another would a child.
They smile at me and keep me warm.
One idea leads to another like steps of stairs.
I built them and ascended, pleased
to have the view from each new landing;
the greater knowledge that came
with each consolidation. Some of these landings
had names – Priest, Teacher, Cardinal.

It was never the name but the knowledge –
the birth of the next idea, the revelation
of the newly swaddled thought. Was it pride?
Perhaps. If so, God has had His joke.
I never thought to rise so high, to be Pope.
I never wanted it – the danger, the exposure.
But oh, there is so much more that shines
from this throne – a whole world of curiosities.
Perhaps God gives a different message
to the church of men. Here's a new idea:
a woman can be Pope. Have you the brain for it?

# THE UNBROKEN LINE

An unbroken line, they say,
like the rope of a friar
circling Christendom, from Peter
to the days of the second coming;
from the agony of the crucifixion
to the coming horror of the anti-Christ,
all kept safe by this stout rope,
this line of Popes.

Or a ladder, if you like,
each rung a man, God's representative,
stretching from the earth onto heaven,
so that mankind can climb to glory.
But I see them standing
shoulder-to-shoulder like a wall,
a barrier to all that is new,
to ideas, to love.

They are a wall holding back
the kingdom of God on earth.
Why else would He have allowed me
this position if not to show
the weakness in their argument,
to teach them humility, acceptance?
But they are men of pride
and will stay behind their wall.

# THE SECRETS OF THE BODY

I look at myself in the mirror
(how strange to have one, how extravagant).
Is this all there is to a woman's body –
small high breasts let free from their binding,
the marks of the cloth still lining the skin;
the soft spoon of the belly;
the thatch of dark beneath;
a boy's hips; legs used to walking?
Is this the great temptation we preach against?
It is nothing. I see no sin in it.
There must be a different way of looking.
So it comes to me – the sin is in the looker.
It's in his own head. It's a man's sin.
But like all else in this man's world,
the blame is shifted, fear driving
the accusation. Look, this pale-skinned
unlovely body, holds the power of creation,
can bring forth life. We are made in God's image:
in this, perhaps women more than men.
Is this the great secret that Eve discovered?
Is this why Adam wanted to leave the Garden?

## WHAT STRANGENESS

What strangeness this is,
to have been so long in the world of men
that I'd forgotten what it is
to be a woman.

I have lived in myself as if I were a man,
making no distinction, acting
with them as they do with each other.
Now this assistant with his green eyes,

his red hair, has flung me out of my mind.
Now I feel my heart speed,
my whole body yearn
for what can only destroy me.

Surely, he has sensed it –
the way I build a path in all I do
to walk with him; the way I lose the stitch
when sewing the hems of my arguments.

Now he has started coming to me
without a weight of work, as if
we are two rivers coursing towards each other,
soon to be engulfed.

## UNLOCKED

I had never properly considered the body
(except my own in disguise). I believed
the corporeal just a vessel for the cerebral;
the cerebral a door to the soul.

I believed it was all in the mind,
that we could think ourselves different,
unlock an idea as bright as a star
and take a step closer to Heaven.

But then that first time we undressed,
I was filled with joy at the sight
of his body, the way it moved and shaped,
the hard wall of his belly,

his member rearing like a stallion.
When we galloped together,
leaping fence after fence in the
wild country of our bed,

I came to see how perfect
the act of union is, how it made us one
and, in that moment, beyond ourselves,
one with everything in creation.

The door to my body has been unlocked.
I have found myself within.

# BREAD (A LOVER'S TALE)

*There was nothing in her reading of the scriptures that suggested*
*transubstantiation would not occur if a woman broke the bread.*

*So she celebrated Mass and found a following that saw freshness*
*in her soft devotion, wanted to receive the Eucharist from her hand.*

*He's like a boy, they said and marveled. What nourishment she gave*
*their souls. They were eating with a saint. When I found out*

*she was a woman, it just seemed right. At first I was afraid to hold her,*
*the longings of my body and my soul now joined as one, I feared*

*I'd damn myself to hell if I should harm her. Yet I find something*
*of the animal in her, an energy for rutting that leaves me drained.*

*She consumes me. This is my body, she says, lifting the Host high.*
*I harden like a colt under my cassock when she tears the bread apart.*

# A LOVE LIKE THIS

I want love that is not just for Christmas
but stays scampering around my heart
through the spring rains, the summer melt,
and the many Christmases that follow.
I want it to mature, I want to take it for walks,
say *fetch* and have it always come back to me.
I want it to sleep in my chamber, to pad along
from one room to the next. I want it to protect me
from all the absences I feel, from loss.
I want it to gaze at me in silent communion,
to wag its tail when I feed it. When I come
home and hang up the pain of my day on a hook,
I want it to leap at me, fill my heart with its barking.

# THE COMING STORM

So now I have a lover and the world is bright.
I am giddy with the joy of it. I'm terrified.
I'm like a child on the back of a wild horse,
excited by its gallop but knowing I will fall.
Does God seek to test me thus?
Oh but this sin's so sweet. Yet surely all love
comes from Him and is, so, good.

The sin is in deceit. If there's a price to pay
it will be for sitting on the chair of Peter.
One thing I have learned: no one is great
or wise or saintly. The most noble in the land
ache and fart, have doubts, accumulate
a heavy sack of sins. My body has been a boat
easy on the sea, believing only calm.
But water's only quiet when asleep.

# I AM

- the Holy Mother of the Church
- who would feed all of her children
- who would preach them from their ignorance
- full-bellied and heavy with love
- the lamb in wolf's clothing
- a spear in the side of the sure
- a cup that only I can drink
- the waddler of halls, an over-fed bishop
- too long in this confinement
- the one who will soon release hurt
- who will make men question their sight
- who would make them question their place
- who will not survive this birthing
- follower of *the Way, the Truth and the Life* *

\* John 14:16

# BIG

As I got big he grew appalled,
began to scourge himself,
cried about the size of our sin,
a mountain flattening his soul.

He whipped himself and said
it was the weakness of the flesh,
not love, that brought us to union.
*God has left me. You led*

*me to His absence.* I answered him,
*He is here, shining,* my hand
on the globe of my belly.
But when I was a month from term

he left – this was his real weakness
of the flesh, his fear of the cardinals,
his back wet with his own urging,
drawing him away like a pack horse.

# AFTERWARDS

Once touched,
she could never feel content —
a sky of stars to wish upon,
the whole black night to melt.

Like a little girl,
she would turn her face up
to be kissed in the dark.

Too long a time has gone by
for me to have stayed in love;
too short yet to forget.

My love has made her a stranger.
She does not even know herself.
Like a moth overpowered by a flame,
she has no beauty left.

# EXPURGATED

I am to be expurgated.
They will make a lie of me.
It was like a miracle. Reversed. My waters
broke as I rode amongst the crowd.
The cardinals would not understand.
*I am with child*, I groaned at them
from the spasm of contraction.
It was my own people
got me off the street. I sometimes
wonder if that was what was meant to be:
that I bear witness through my birthing
to a universal church. The Cardinals worry
that I am an omen and are afraid
to kill me. They have decided
to close me into a nunnery.
They have washed their minds clean.

# CANDLE

Sometimes I wonder that I can go on. I feel like a candle
spluttering in the last pool of myself. The sisters here treat me
like a saint, my great age seeming to be a daily miracle.

Already I am half gone from the world – hours or days go by,
my mind joining the one end to the other but missing
what's in-between, leapfrogging patches of my life

as if eager for its end. Sometimes it comes back –
the way knowledge made a drunkard out of me, so that I always
had a book hidden somewhere and if my hands were empty

of writing for too long, they'd shake. I had a visitor today –
or was it yesterday – a Cardinal in scarlet robes.
He came and bowed to me. He kissed my hand, called me Mother.

Sometimes I miss the girlhood that I absented and think
that I never was a woman. Sometimes I remember being in love and
know that once I was and so burn a little brighter for an hour.

## ACKNOWLEDGEMENTS

Some of these poems have previously been published in PN *Review* (UK) and *Seminary Ridge Review* (USA). I would like to thank Todd Swift for believing in these poems and publishing them. I would also like to thank my son, Aidan Dullaghan, for the artwork.

Printed by Libri Plureos GmbH in Hamburg, Germany